The Big Book of Baby Names from Italy

Girls

Abriana
Addolorata
Adele
Adelina
Adrina
Agata
Agnella
Agnesca
Agnesina
Agnola
Agnolla
Agnolle
Aida
Aidy
Alda
Alessa
Alessandra
Alessi
Alessia
Alice

Allegra
Allegretta
Aloe
Alvara
Amadea
Amadora
Amalfey
Amalfi
Amalia
Amara
Amaranta
Amata
Ambra
Ambrosi
Amedea
Amelda
Ameriga
Amidala
Analia
Andolina
Andrea
Anete
Angela

Angelica
Angelina
Anita
Anna
Annabella
Annunciata
Annunziata
Annunziate
Anonciada
Antonella
Anunciacion
Anunciata
Anunziata
Aradia
Aria
Ariana
Arianna
Armani
Armina
Aryana
Aryanna
Asia
Assisi

Aurora
Avellina
Azzurra
Bambalina
Bambi
Bambie
Bambina
Bamby
Barbarella
Batista
Beatrice
Belenda
Bella
Belladonna
Bellanca
Bellezza
Bellini
Benedetta
Benita
Beonca
Beretta
Bernardetta
Beronia

Bertrona
Betta
Bettina
Beyonca
Bianca
Biancha
Bianey
Bianka
Bice
Bionca
Bionda
Blanca
Blancha
Bona
Bonfilia
Brandy
Brava
Bria
Briella
Brigida
Brio
Bruna
Brune

Brunetta
Buona
Byanca
Cadenza
Calogera
Cameo
Camila
Camilla
Cammeo
Campana
Candella
Capella
Capree
Capreece
Capri
Capriana
Caprice
Capricia
Caprise
Cara
Carabel
Carabell
Carabella

Carabelle
Carin
Carina
Carissa
Carla
Carlina
Carlota
Carlotta
Carmela
Caro
Carrabelle
Caterina
Cavalli
Cecilia
Celestina
Celinka
Cettina
Chezarina
Chiara
Chiarina
Chipriana
Chiprianna
Chloe

Ciana
Ciandra
Cianna
Cinetta
Cinzia
Cipriana
Cipriane
Ciprianna
Cira
Claretta
Clarice
Clarina
Coda
Como
Concetta
Concettina
Concilia
Condoleeza
Consolata
Constantia
Contessa
Coretta
Cosetta

Cosima

Cosma

Cristina

Cynzia

Cypriana

Cyprienne

Dahna

Dahnya

Daniella

Delfina

Dicembre

Diva

Domani

Domenica

Dominica

Domitilla

Donalie

Donatella

Donella

Donelle

Donica

Donielle

Donisha

Donna
Donna-Marie
Donnalee
Donnalyn
Donnella
Donnelle
Donnetta
Donni
Donnisse
Donya
Drucilla
Edda
Edetta
Editta
Edvige
Elda
Eleanora
Elena
Eleonara
Eleonora
Elettra
Elia
Elisa

Elisabetta
Elizabetta
Eloisa
Elvera
Emanuele
Emilia
Emiliana
Emily
Emma
Emmanuella
Enrica
Enricka
Enricketta
Enriqueta
Enriquette
Epifania
Ermenegilda
Eroica
Eroiqua
Eroique
Etta
Eva
Fabiana

Fabiola
Fabricia
Fabrienne
Fabriqua
Fabritzia
Fabrizia
Fauci
Fausta
Federica
Felice
Fella
Fendi
Fenicia
Fernanda
Ferrari
Fia
Fiamma
Fiammetta
Filide
Filippina
Fillippa
Filomena
Fina

Fiora
Fiorella
Fiorentina
Fiorenza
Franca
Francesca
Gabriela
Gabriella
Gaetana
Gaetane
Gaia
Galilea
Garbo
Gelsomina
Gemma
Genevra
Genoa
Genoveffa
Genoveva
Genoviva
Geoconda
Geonna
Geovana

Geovanna
Gessica
Ghita
Gia
Giacinta
Giada
Giana
Gianella
Gianetta
Gianina
Gianna
Giannina
Giannine
Giavanna
Gina
Ginara
Ginata
Ginerva
Ginetta
Ginette
Ginevra
Ginnette
Gioconda

Gioia
Gionna
Giordana
Giorgia
Giovana
Giovanna
Giralda
Giuditta
Giugnia
Giulia
Giuliana
Giulietta
Giuseppa
Giuseppina
Giustina
Gratia
Gratiana
Grazia
Graziana
Graziella
Graziosa
Greta
Guglielma

Guida
Gulielma
Hagne
Heroica
Himalda
Honora
Honorata
Idalia
Ilaria
Illeana
Imalda
Imelda
Irene
Isabel
Isabella
Isabetta
Isotta
Itala
Italia
Izabella
Izola
Jacobella
Janina

Jaquetta
Jeeanima
Jelsomina
Jeoconda
Jiacintha
Jolanda
Josefina
Jovanne
Justina
Kara
Karissa
Katarina
Katina
Laguna
Lanza
Laretta
Larretta
Laudonia
Laurenza
Lauretta
Lavanda
Lave
Leandra

Leggra
Legra
Lelia
Leona
Leone
Leonora
Leretta
Letizia
Lia
Librina
Lido
Liliana
Lilla
Lina
Linda
Liona
Lorenza
Loreta
Loretta
Lotta
Lowretta
Lozano
Luca

Lucia
Luciana
Luciella
Lucrezia
Ludovica
Luisa
Luna
Mabilia
Madalene
Maddalena
Madona
Madonna
Mafalda
Magenta
Maggia
Mancuso
Marcella
Marconi
Margherita
Maria
Mariabella
Mariella
Marietta

Marisa
Marsala
Marta
Martedi
Martina
Marzia
Massima
Matelda
Matilde
Mattea
Mea
Melissa
Menichina
Messina
Mia
Micaela
Michele
Michelle
Mila
Milana
Mirabella
Mirella
Miriam

Mirra
Mistico
Miuccia
Mona
Monaco
Narissa
Naryssa
Natala
Natale
Natalia
Nedda
Nericcia
Nerissa
Nerola
Neroli
Nerolia
Nerolie
Neroly
Neryssa
Nicia
Nico
Nicola
Nicole

Nilda
Nillda
Ninetta
Noemi
Nunciata
Nunzia
Orabella
Orella
Organza
Oriana
Ornella
Orsa
Orsina
Orsola
Ortensa
Ortensia
Ortensija
Ortensya
Ottavia
Pamina
Paola
Paolina
Pasquelina

Patina
Patrizia
Pazienza
Perlita
Pertessa
Petronilla
Phebe
Pia
Piccolo
Piera
Pierina
Pietra
Pippa
Placida
Po
Prima
Primavera
Quorra
Rachele
Raffaele
Raffaella
Raimona
Raimonda

Raphaela
Ravenna
Rebecca
Renata
Rialta
Ricarda
Ricci
Ricciarda
Rin
Rina
Risa
Riviera
Rizzo
Robbia
Rochelle
Rocio
Roma
Romalda
Romana
Romanadia
Romancia
Romannea
Rome

Romelia
Romilda
Romina
Romma
Rosa
Rosana
Rosemund
Roseta
Rosetta
Rosina
Rosmunda
Rossa
Ruffina
Rufina
Russa
Sancia
Sandra
Santa
Santina
Santuzza
Sara
Sarafina
Sardinia

Sarita
Saveria
Scianna
Scirocco
Serafina
Serenella
Sicily
Sidonia
Siena
Sienna
Sigismonda
Sigismunda
Sigmonda
Sigmunda
Silva
Silvana
Silvia
Silvina
Simona
Simonetta
Sipriana
Sipriane
Siprianne

Sistine
Sofia
Speranca
Speranza
Stamatina
Stefania
Sypriana
Syprianne
Tanaquil
Tea
Tekla
Telma
Teodora
Teofila
Teresa
Teresina
Terina
Terra
Tersa
Terza
Tessa
Titian
Toma

Tomassa
Tosca
Traviata
Trilby
Tristessa
Tutti
Uberrta
Uberta
Ubertha
Urbana
Vahnda
Valeria
Vallea
Vallombrosa
Valombrosa
Vannda
Varenna
Vedetta
Vedette
Velia
Venecia
Venetia
Venezia

Venice
Verdi
Verona
Via
Vicenza
Vincenza
Vinceta
Viola
Violetta
Vita
Vitalia
Vittoria
Vivia
Viviana
Vohnda
Volta
Vonda
Yacinta
Yacintha
Ymelda
Yuberta
Zappa
Zelmira

Zerlina
Zeta
Zoela
Zola
Zolia

Boys

Abrahamo
Abramo
Acciai
Achilleo
Adagio
Adolfo
Adriano
Agatho
Agnolo
Agostino
Agosto
Alberico
Aldo

Aldon
Aldus
Alessandro
Alessi
Alessio
Alexius
Alfio
Alfonso
Alfredo
Alldo
Alonzo
Alphonsus
Alvino
Amadeo
Amando
Amato
Ambrogio
Ambrosi
Amedeo
Americo
Americus
Amerigo
Amerika

Ameriko
Amerikus
Amilcare
Anastagio
Anatolio
Andrea
Angelo
Angelos
Anselmo
Antioch
Antiochos
Antiochus
Antioco
Antonio
Araldo
Ardian
Arduino
Aretino
Armando
Armani
Armano
Armino
Arnald

Arnaldo
Arnaud
Arnauld
Arnault
Arnoldo
Arnolfo
Aroldo
Arrigo
Arturo
Attilio
Aurelio
Avellino
Baggio
Baldasarre
Baldassare
Baldwin
Barnardo
Barrucio
Battista
Battiste
Bautiste
Bellarmine
Bellarmino

Bello
Bellveder
Bellvedere
Bellvidere
Belveder
Belvedere
Belvider
Belvidere
Benedetto
Beniamino
Benigno
Benito
Benjamino
Benvenuto
Benvolio
Bernadino
Bertoldo
Biaggio
Biagio
Biondello
Borachio
Borromeo
Bosco

Brahvo
Brando
Braulio
Bravo
Bravvo
Brio
Brizio
Bronze
Buono
Cajetan
Cajetano
Calogero
Calogeros
Calvino
Capri
Carlino
Carlo
Carmello
Carmelo
Carmine
Caro
Carolo
Caruso

Cassio
Cavalli
Ceasario
Cecilio
Cedro
Celesto
Cellini
Cesare
Cesco
Chidro
Chirico
Christian
Cidro
Cielo
Cipriano
Ciriaco
Cirillo
Ciro
Cirocco
Cirrillo
Clelio
Clemente
Coda

Columbano
Columbo
Como
Cono
Constantino
Constanzo
Corrado
Cosimo
Cosmo
Damiano
Damone
Daniel
Daniele
Dante
Darin
Dario
Davide
Deangelo
Demarco
Demario
Deusdedit
Diego
Dino

Dionigi
Domani
Domenico
Donatelli
Donatello
Donati
Donato
Dontaye
Donte
Dontey
Donus
Draco
Drago
Duran
Durante
Ecedro
Ecidro
Edmondo
Edoardo
Egidio
Eigidio
Elia
Elio

Eliseo
Elmo
Emanuele
Emidio
Emiliano
Emilio
Enea
Ennio
Enrico
Enzio
Enzo
Epifanio
Erasto
Ercole
Ercolo
Eriberto
Ermanno
Erminio
Esidor
Esidore
Esidoro
Esidro
Ettore

Eugenio
Eustachio
Ezio
Fabbro
Fabian
Fabiano
Fabio
Fabrizio
Fabroni
Falito
Faro
Fauci
Fausto
Fedele
Federico
Federigo
Fendi
Feo
Ferrando
Ferrari
Fico
Fidelio
Fiero

Filberte
Filippo
Fio
Fiorello
Fiorenzo
Flavio
Fleance
Floritzel
Fortino
Francesco
Franco
Gabriel
Gaetan
Gaetano
Gaeton
Galileo
Gaspare
Gasparo
Gavino
Genaro
Gennarius
Gennaro
Gennaros

Geno
Genovese
Geofredo
Geona
Georgino
Geovani
Geovanney
Geovanni
Geovanny
Geovany
Gerardo
Geremia
Gerodi
Gerome
Geronimo
Giacob
Giacomo
Gian
Giancarlo
Gianney
Gianni
Giannino
Gianny

Gideone
Gino
Gioacchino
Gioachino
Gioele
Giona
Giordano
Giorgio
Giosia
Giosue
Giotto
Giovan
Giovani
Giovanni
Giovanno
Giovanny
Giovel
Giovell
Giovonni
Girlado
Girolamo
Gitano
Giuliano

Giulio
Giuseppe
Giustinian
Giustiniano
Giustino
Goffredo
Gracian
Graciano
Gratiano
Graziano
Greco
Gregorio
Gualtier
Gualtiero
Guglielmo
Guido
Guistino
Guntero
Gustavo
Herberto
Heriberto
Herinomos
Heronimo

Hieronimo
Hieronymus
Hisidro
Honorius
Hormisdas
Hortensio
Ilario
Indro
Innocent
Innocenty
Innocenzio
Inocencio
Inocenzio
Inocenzo
Ippolito
Isaia
Isidro
Italo
Jacopo
Januario
Jeno
Jeronimo
Jeronimus

Jino
Jovanney
Jovanno
Kajetan
Kajetano
Kalogerus
Karmello
Karmelo
Kosmo
Lanz
Lanza
Lapo
Lazaro
Lazzaro
Leandro
Leo
Leonardo
Leone
Leonello
Leonida
Leonzio
Lionzio
Lodovico

Lombardi
Lorenzo
Lozano
Luca
Lucca
Luciano
Lucio
Ludovic
Luigi
Maggio
Mancuso
Manfredo
Mano
Manuel
Manzu
Marcello
Marciano
Marco
Marconi
Mariano
Mario
Martelli
Martino

Maso
Massimo
Mateo
Matteo
Mattia
Maurilio
Maurizio
Mauro
Maury
Maximiliano
Maximo
Meo
Mercury
Messala
Messina
Michelangelo
Michele
Modesto
Monaco
Morandi
Napoleon
Nardo
Natale

Nataniele
Nathan
Nazario
Nek
Nevio
Nico
Nicola
Nicolo
Nicolò
Nino
Nuncio
Nunzio
Oliviero
Onofre
Onofredo
Onofrio
Onofrius
Onophrio
Oratio
Orazio
Orfeo
Orlando
Orsino

Otello
Othello
Ottavio
Ottone
Paco
Pancrazio
Paolo
Paris
Pasquale
Patrizio
Pellegrino
Pepe
Philario
Piccolo
Pierluigi
Piero
Pietro
Pino
Pirro
Pisano
Placido
Po
Porfirio

Preemo
Premo
Prime
Primo
Proculeius
Prospero
Rafaele
Raffaele
Raffaello
Raimondo
Ranieri
Remo
Renato
Renz
Renzo
Riccardo
Ricci
Ricciardo
Ricco
Rico
Rinaldo
Rizzo
Roberto

Rocco
Roche
Rochus
Rocko
Rocky
Rodolfo
Rolando
Romano
Rome
Romeo
Romolo
Roque
Roreto
Rosario
Rudolpho
Ruggerio
Ruggero
Ruggiero
Ruperto
Russo
Salamone
Salvatore
Salvatorio

Salvio
Samuel
Samuele
Sandrino
Sandro
Sansone
Santa
Santino
Santo
Sanzio
Saverio
Savino
Scianna
Secondo
Serafino
Sergio
Sesto
Severino
Severo
Sigefriedo
Silvano
Silvestro
Silvio

Simone
Sisto
Solanio
Stefano
Taddeo
Tancredo
Tasso
Tempo
Teo
Teodosio
Terancio
Terenciano
Thadeo
Thomas
Timeo
Tino
Tiziano
Tomasso
Tommaso
Trey
Tristano
Tullio
Tuomo

Tutti
Ubert
Uberto
Ugo
Ulisse
Ulrico
Umberto
Ursel
Ursino
Ursins
Ursinus
Urso
Ursus
Valentino
Valentio
Valerius
Varenna
Venetziano
Veneziano
Venezio
Venturo
Verdi
Vesuvio

Vicenzo
Vincenzio
Vincenzo
Vinicio
Vitalian
Vito
Vittorio
Vitus
Vivaldo
Volta
Xanto
Yovanney
Yovanni
Yovanny
Zanebono
Zanipolo
Zappa

Made in the USA
Las Vegas, NV
07 February 2025